Kings Landing

Kings Landing
Country Life in Early Canada

Photographs by Wayne Barrett

Introduction by George MacBeath

Toronto
OXFORD UNIVERSITY PRESS
1979

Dedicated to all who created Kings Landing

Acknowledgements
My thanks are due to many people for their help and
encouragement, but especially to Dr George Mac-
Beath, Mr Douglas Cole, the staff of Kings Landing
Historical Settlement, the Oxford University Press,
and to my wife Anne, for her patience and insight.

WB

The Publishers wish to thank the staff and manage-
ment of Kings Landing Historical Settlement for their
unfailing help and guidance, without which this book
would not have been possible.

Canadian Cataloguing in Publication Data
Barrett, Wayne.
Kings Landing

ISBN 0-19-540301-0

1. Kings Landing, N.B. - Description - Views.
2. Historic sites - New Brunswick - Kings
Landing - Pictorial works. I. MacBeath, George.
II. Title.

FC2465.K5.B37   917.15'51   C79-094281-X
F1042.8.B37

Designed by FORTUNATO AGLIALORO

© Oxford University Press (Canadian Branch) 1979
ISBN 0-19-540301-0
1234-2109
Printed in Hong Kong by
EVERBEST PRINTING COMPANY LIMITED

Introduction

Almost everyone, I suspect, will have looked at the pictures in this book before even glancing at these introductory remarks. I know I could not have resisted doing so! Wayne Barrett's pictorial views are altogether delightful, the more so because he has exercised his artistic license to present us with a collection of colour photographs that, taken together, give us both a pictorial representation of the reality of Kings Landing Historical Settlement and an album of central New Brunswick in the nineteenth century. The effect of this is to pay Kings Landing the ultimate compliment: to show that the settlement truly represents the way of life of an era.

By selecting and capturing moments from the life at Kings Landing, Mr Barrett has made us aware of how he sees the special character of the place. In a similar way, its originators were forced to use historical license in choosing from among many old buildings in the St John valley those that should be preserved in an outdoor museum setting. The liberties taken in both cases somehow bring into focus the very essence of early New Brunswick.

It was back in 1963 that the first evaluation of the concept of an open-air museum was undertaken. That was the year when New Brunswick, with the aid of the federal government, determined to set about solving the growing need for electricity by constructing a large hydro dam on the St John River at Mactaquac. The river behind the dam would be raised some two hundred feet, flooding the low-lying part of the valley for a distance of fifty-five miles. This would result in extensive and tragic loss to the upriver farms and hamlets, including some of the valley's most fertile land.

Despite the bitter opposition engendered, the heartbreak of disrupted lives, and the prospect of a heritage destroyed, the decision to proceed with construction of the dam was confirmed. Once it became evident that there was no way of stopping the valley's flooding, it was determined to make the best of the situation. We would save as many of the buildings as we could and relocate them to form part of a modern re-creation of a historical settlement, to be called Kings Landing–a name adopted to suggest a

5

Loyalist origin and a riverside location. We realized that this would be somewhat contrived, an inadequate representation of the way of life that had been rooted in the valley for generations, but it seemed clear that any such reservations would be outweighed by the advantages of preserving for people's enjoyment and instruction an invaluable link with the past.

The cultural story of that part of the province goes back to prehistoric times, when Malecite Indians inhabited the region. For many centuries the St John River served as an important waterway. The Indians who first used the river were in time joined by French, Acadian, and British travellers. Until little more than a century and a half ago, the St John River was the main inland route between Quebec and the Maritimes.

British control of the river was established in 1758, when its valley was still a largely untouched wilderness, rich in furs, timber, and fish. What little attempt at settlement there had been up to this time was transitory; but now permanent habitations began to spring up, tiny hamlets being first established at Maugerville and at the estuary.

After 1783 some ten thousand settlers came to make new homes for themselves along the St John and its tributaries, and in the city they built at the river's mouth. These people were Loyalist refugees, men and women who had remained loyal to the Crown during the American Revolution and at the end had been forced to flee their homes. With their arrival the St John valley– inland for over a hundred miles– became a hive of activity.

Among this great band of hopeful newcomers to the valley were soldiers of several recently disbanded Loyalist regiments. To the area where Kings Landing is now located came officers and men of the King's American Dragoons, who had been given land in recognition of their service during the Revolutionary War. This, then, was the beginning of that successful settlement endeavour which Kings Landing seeks to depict.

With time the frontier wilderness yielded to their hard work, however reluctantly. Cleared lands, buildings, and fields under cultivation came to be a familiar sight to river travellers. As time passed, the early settlers were joined by others– principally from Ireland, Scotland, England, and the United States– along with a few who had first lived 'down-river'.

It is not difficult to understand why the great majority of these new arrivals chose to settle on the banks of the St John and its tributary branches. With no roads, the river made travel relatively easy, in both winter and summer, all the way from Saint John to Edmundston; the substantial traffic it carried was the lifeblood of the inhabitants of the valley. The dominant effect of the river is clearly evident in existing plans of early valley communities. They are shown to have been remarkably drawn out, with the earliest buildings stretching along the banks. Most of the later arrivals, who were townspeople, constructed homes beside the roads that came to be built parallel to the river or running away from it to link up with the back settlements.

In developing the overall concept to be followed in creating Kings Landing, decisions about its location, size, and make-up had to be made. Our research revealed that, to recapture in a truly authentic way the unique nature of our first New Brunswick river settlements, it was essential that this historical re-creation be located very near the water, with the oldest buildings appropriately sited on the river's edge. The rich farmland sloping up gently from the water would remain the dominant feature of the landscape.

It was important to have a stream nearby to provide the power to operate a sawmill. The growth of early communities often depended on such a facility, since it provided not only lumber required for construction, but also jobs for new settlers. Men were needed to operate the mill, to cut timber in the backlands to feed it, and to transport the finished product to markets. In turn, the services of such craftsmen as carpenters, blacksmiths, cobblers, and millwrights were required, and these people would inevitably be

attracted as residents to the tiny marketing centres that were evolving. With the coming of still more families, it followed that such necessary additions to the community as a general store, a church, a school, and an inn were built.

These, then, are the broad factors that were observed in laying out the site and choosing the buildings to be used in creating Kings Landing Historical Settlement. Buildings were selected because they were representative of the region's architectural legacy and because they would group well to form a settlement. They came almost entirely from the headpond area. Yet we were fortunate in finding a range of styles, from the home of a well-to-do merchant to the dwelling of a modest worker, from the work of a sophisticated builder to that of a carpenter. What excitement there was in relocating these buildings! The majority were carried on a specially constructed trailer, those from across the river being brought over during the winter on a carefully prepared road made on the ice. The Long house was floated in by barge, from its original location a few miles down-river, in an atmosphere of adventure and high excitement. The stone structure we call the Jones house was dismantled at Prince William and moved, stone by coded stone, to its present site for reassembly.

It was determined that the role most of the houses would be called upon to play in the new settlement should be based on their actual history. Some modification was necessary to fit a house to its Kings Landing setting. Since each of the building groupings was to be restored to a different date in the past, it would be possible to illustrate the changes in type and way of life throughout the nineteenth century.

The boats that came and went on the St John were a vital part of the everyday scene. Many years ago I wrote about a sailing vessel that once was a common sight on the river but had long been forgotten. It was called a woodboat, from the most usual cargo it carried, although it also transported people and farm produce to Saint John, returning up-river with manufactured goods. No craft quite like it was to be found anywhere else in the world, since its generic design evolved here because of the particular needs to be served. Nearly five hundred of these boats had operated on the river, and it seemed logical to associate one with Kings Landing, which would have been dependent on a river-borne trade. Using the tools and methods of the last century, an authentic replica of a twenty-ton woodboat of the 1830s was constructed right at the settlement. The launching of the *Brunswick Lion*, as she was named, was a particularly satisfying event, since it meant that another unique part of New Brunswick's heritage had been given three-dimensional form.

The pages that follow show the presence of many costumed children at the settlement, and this needs a word of explanation. Some of these younger citizens are the children of employees, while others are a part of the Visiting Cousins program. All become totally immersed in settlement life by actually living there. Although they sleep at night in modern quarters just outside the historical area, during the day they are given a house to visit and are treated as the visiting relatives of the people who 'live' in that house. Clothed in period costume, they help with the chores at their historic house and spend part of each day in the settlement school. They are also allowed to work in the sawmill, carpenter's shop, smithy, and on the farm. Recreation comes in the form of games, picnics, fishing at the millpond, and handicrafts. This unique program provides an unforgettable experience in living history for the children, and they in turn lend their own charm to the total environment of the settlement.

The historical settlement of Kings Landing is nearly four hundred acres in extent and comprises some seventy buildings. Close to ten million dollars have been invested in this worthwhile rural heritage project, the most ambitious one of its kind ever undertaken in New Brunswick. It first opened to the public on a limited basis in 1970, and officially in 1974 – eight years after the start of work.

Kings Landing could not have been accomplished without the dedication of many people, whose contributions were manifold. In the beginning there were those who laboured to clear and prepare the site, architects and historians who evaluated the structures and tended to their moving and restoration. Then there were the curators who collected artefacts and arranged the furnishing of interiors to an earlier period, the experts who saw to the landscaping and gardening, the conservators who repaired and restored the several thousand items needed in the homes and outbuildings, the costume designers and seamstresses, the carpenters and painters, and so many, many others who made their special contributions. They all had a vision of what Kings Landing should be; for this reason they made a personal and lasting contribution to its special character.

From its conception and birth, through its infancy and early years, Kings Landing has grown and, like a maturing adult, is now a unique entity – something more than the sum of the parts it was given. Even those of us most closely related to it can find in this book surprise and discovery in the reality that has evolved.

GEORGE MAC BEATH

1 This replica of the 1837 wood-boat *Brunswick Lion* is safely moored in Courser Cove. Her bulldog bow and lack of head-sails are two of the distinguishing features of this local craft. In the background are the Long and Lint houses.

2 The buildings of Kings Landing are linked by winding dirt
roads such as this one, which
runs past the 1845 Long house.

3 Visiting Cousins gathering daisies from the Morehouse field to decorate the table for Sunday's dinner.

4 Traditional plants in the Ingraham flower garden provide a feast for the eye.

5 Hoeing in one of the fertile fields that stretch gently back from the river's edge.

6 St Mark's is a country church typical of the Anglican chapels that are still a familiar site in the Valley.

7 Wagons such as this sloven at the Joslin farm are used to carry visitors over part of the settlement's roads, which extend for over a mile along the river.

8 A sundial is the focal point of the formal garden in front of the 1840 Ingraham house. Perhaps the most splendid of the Kings Landing buildings, it stands on the bank of the St John River.

9 This rare octagonal privy, which is now in the backyard of the Ingraham house, was built only a few miles from Kings Landing in 1795 by Chief Justice Saunders.

10 Tending the roses lining the front walk of the 1867 Perley house. A dwelling appropriate to a well-to-do storekeeper, it typifies the steeply pitched front gable and tasteful ornamental detail associated with mid-Victorian homes.

11 Sunlight streams into the entrance hall of the residence built by the Loyalist Daniel Morehouse.

12

13

14

15

The interiors of these homes depict the manners and circumstances of their owners:

12 the Ingraham dining room
13 the Joslin parlour
14 the Jones dining room – with stencilled floor
15 the drawing room of the Long house

16 The Ingrahams take a few moments of relaxation before tea in their drawing room, re-created as it would have been in 1840.

17 Washing up in the Jones house kitchen. Some domestic chores have changed little in a hundred years.

18 Father and daughter after a meal that has been prepared over the open fire in the 1790s kitchen of the Smith house.

Baking day at Kings Landing settlement:

19 the 1870 Hagerman pantry

20 the Hagerman kitchen

21 the Ingraham pantry

22 the Joslin kitchen

23 Thankful blessings for what the land has provided –
noonday meal in the Ingraham kitchen.

24

25

26

27

Scenes from bedrooms of the past:
24 a girl at a desk in the Morehouse residence
25 making up the canopied bed in the Ingraham daughter's room
26 the spinning corner in a bedroom of the Jones house
27 the boys' room in the Ingraham house

28 A quiet corner in the upper hall of the Jones house, restored in the style of the 1830s.

29 Women in the settlement at a quilting bee in the Morehouse family room.
The bridal-wreath pattern was a popular one in New Brunswick a century ago.

30 Young women weaving on a floor-loom in the attic of the Huestis house.
Filling the family's need for clothing was important work.

31 Young girls learn old ways – making butter at the Joslin farm.

32 As autumn approaches, one of the many preparations for winter on the
Joslin farm includes the shelling of beans.

33 Interior of the Perley store, with its range of goods of the 1870s. Thousands of
items were kept on hand, providing a delight for sight and smell.

34 Much can be learned of nineteenth - century life from the many items to be
found in a country store.

35 The teacher takes pleasure in sharing a good story with a favourite pupil.

36 Students from the Visiting Cousins program struggle with their Roman numerals in this one-room schoolhouse. Built at Queensbury near Kings Landing in 1835, it can accommodate only twenty-three pupils.

37 Children living close to nature's wilderness experience the wonder of living creatures.

38 Feeding the ducks behind the Perley house.

39 Fishing for trout off the Jones' wharf on a midsummer afternoon.

40 A sloven passes over the
1860-type bridge of round
cedar logs that spans the Peter
Smith brook.

41 The apple trees in the Joslin pasture yield a rich harvest for man *and* beast.

42 Oxen stand patiently as the men pitch hay on the wagon beside the 1850 Huestis house.

43

44

45

46

Routine tasks, no longer familiar in a modern world:
43 sharpening a scythe at the Long ox-barn
44 shaving shingles beside the Smith house
45 repair work in the wheelwright shop
46 greasing a wagon on the Joslin farm

47 At work in the mill-yard, men are loading newly sawn planks on the horse-drawn sloven.

48

49

50

51

Scenes inside the water powered sawmill:
48 handmade wooden gears transmit power from the waterwheel to the saw
49 bagging sawdust
50 sharpening the six-foot up-and-down cutting blade
51 adjusting the carriage that inches the log forward with each stroke of the saw

52 Greasing the hub of the twenty-one-foot overshot waterwheel. The flow of water from the head pond is controlled in the flume.

54

55

53 Inside the smithy the black-smith pumps the bellows to heat his forge. His role was an important one in rural community life of the nineteenth century; he could do everything from shoeing a horse to fashioning a door latch.

Work for a summer's day:
54 oiling the harness
55 whittling
56 shoeing a horse outside the smithy
57 an ox, supported in a sling, has a hoof tended to in the Long barn

56

57

58 Militia training required mastery of the flintlock musket.

59 His musket cleaned and polished, a veteran sergeant remembers the Revolutionary War.

60 The apple-cider cart waits for customers outside the Kings Theatre. In the distance is a woodboat sailing before the wind.

61 A game of 'blind-man's-buff'.

62 Passing the Kileen cabin on the way to the militia muster. This 1830s one-room pioneer home is in a small clearing in the woods at the edge of the settlement.

63 A prominent landmark is the Ingraham house, whose graceful Georgian style of architecture adds its own unique appeal to Kings Landing.

64 Harvesting turnips, which were a winter staple for man and farm animals alike.

65 A split-cedar snake fence encloses a field on the Joslin farm.

66 Fall plowing prepares a field for spring planting. In the background barns, houses, the church, and the store line the settlement's main road.

67 Tidying up the harness in the Joslin horse barn – a daily routine.

68 A typical sawmill of 1830,
with its water barrels for fire
protection lining the roof. Such
mills were at the very heart of
the economic life of the
timber-rich valley area.

69 Enjoying the cool smoke
from a long-stemmed clay pipe
typical of the 1800s.

70 All dressed up, the crowd gathers to listen to a perform-ance at the Agricultural Fair.

Settlement portraits:
71 an 1820s-style straw bonnet
frames a pretty face
72 a timeless picture of father
and daughter

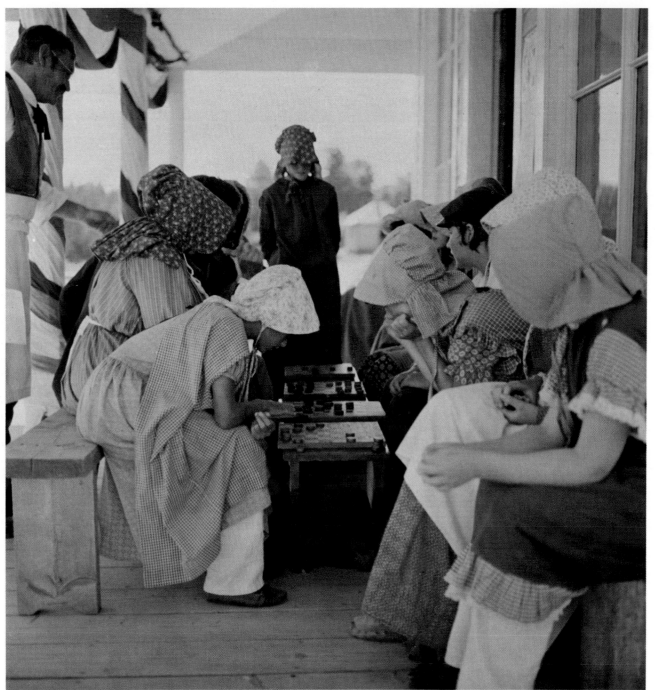

73 Youngsters on the veranda of the Perley General Store are engrossed in a checkers competition during the Agricultural fair.

74 Experienced hands spin wool on a walking wheel.

75 Preserves put down for winter use.

76 A family enjoys an evening meal at the comfortable Kings Head Inn.

77 Preparing for a harvest
service at St Mark's Chapel-
of-Ease. The original wall sten-
ciling of the 1860s has been carefully replicated.

78 A cool tankard of ale at the
end of a hard day: the pub at
the Kings Head.

79 Andrew Joslin developed his farm at the Barony in the late 1790s. The house and outbuildings are restored to depict the 1860 working farm of his grandson, William Joslin.

80 Woodboats, like the *Brunswick Lion*, shown here at the Jones wharf, some-
times carried passengers as well as freight between the communities that dotted
the St John River below Fredericton.

81 'Johnny Woodboat', known as the workhorse of the river, was important as a trading link between settlements on the St John.

82 The crew hoist the mainsail of the *Brunswick Lion* as the vessel prepares to set off down-river.

JOSEPH HOLYOKE PROP.
LICENCED TO SELL WINES AND BEERS

83 Despite the waves of temperance which swept New Brunswick in the mid-nineteenth century, inns such as the Kings Head continued to be regularly frequented.

84 Churchgoers arrive by sleigh for the morning service at St Mark's Chapel.

85 A horse-drawn sleigh approaches the Perley house.

86 Preparing for a festive season: stringing cranberries at the Kings Head Inn.

87 The Morehouse and Ingraham homes and outbuildings stand out against a landscape covered by the first snowfall of winter.

88 Cheviot sheep stand in the Jones barn.

89 *(overleaf)* Early morning on the bridge as another workday begins.